D1710887

My Body Does Strange Stuff!

What Happens When I Throw Up?

By Greg Roza

Gareth Stevens
Publishing

Please visit our website, www.garethstevens.com. For a free color catalog of all our high-quality books, call toll free 1-800-542-2595 or fax 1-877-542-2596.

Library of Congress Cataloging-in-Publication Data

Roza, Greg.
What happens when I throw up / by Greg Roza.
p. cm. — (My body does strange stuff)
Includes index.
ISBN 978-1-4339-9353-4 (pbk.)
ISBN 978-1-4339-9354-1 (6-Pack)
ISBN 978-1-4339-9352-7 (library binding)
1. Digestion — Juvenile literature. 2. Vomiting — Juvenile literature. 3. Nausea — Juvenile literature. 4. Gastrointestinal system —Juvenile literature. I. Roza, Greg. II. Title.
QP145.R69 2014
612.3—dc23

Published in 2014 by
Gareth Stevens Publishing
111 East 14th Street, Suite 349
New York, NY 10003

Designer: Michael J. Flynn
Editor: Greg Roza

Photo credits: Cover, p. 1 Image Source/Getty Images; p. 5 Sharon Dominick/ Photodisc/Getty Images; p. 7 CLIPAREA|Custom media/Getty Images; p. 9 prudkov/ Getty Images; p. 11 Nick Koudis/Photodisc/Getty Images; p. 13 Handout/Getty Images News/Getty Images; p. 15 marco mayet/Shutterstock.com; p. 17 Juriah Mosin/Shutterstock.com; p. 18 315 studio by khunaspix/Shutterstock.com; p. 21 Steve Winter/National Geographic/Getty Images.

Printed in the United States of America

CPSIA compliance information: Batch #CS13GS: For further information contact Gareth Stevens, New York, New York at 1-800-542-2595.

Contents

Boldface words appear in the glossary.

I'm Gonna Be Sick!

Throwing up is the emptying of the stomach, or tummy, through the mouth. It usually starts with a funny feeling in your stomach. You start to feel dizzy, and your stomach starts rumbling. Hopefully, you make it to the bathroom before...BARF!

5

Body Works

Nerves bring messages from all over your body to your brain. Sometimes the **digestive system** tells the brain that something is wrong. If you're ill or maybe really dizzy, your brain may tell your stomach to empty itself. That's when you throw up.

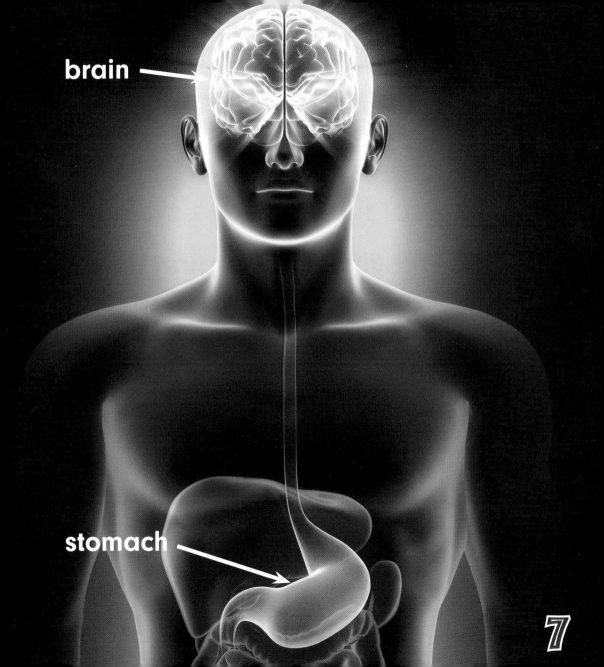

brain

stomach

7

After you chew your food, the **muscles** of the digestive system keep it moving in one direction... most of the time. If you're ill, the brain might tell those muscles to push the food back out of your mouth. Yuck!

9

What's in It?

Vomit is made up of half-digested food. That means it was not fully broken down in the stomach. After throwing up, it's not uncommon to see the food you had recently eaten! Vomit also contains bile, which is a dark green **fluid** that helps digest food.

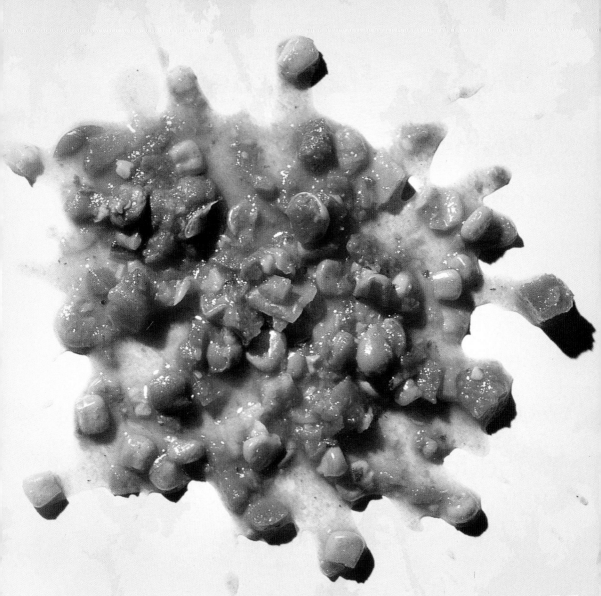

11

Why Do We Throw Up?

Germs called bacteria are the most common reason for throwing up. These tiny creatures are so small we need a microscope to see them. Bacteria can get into our digestive system when we eat bad food. They can cause us to feel sick.

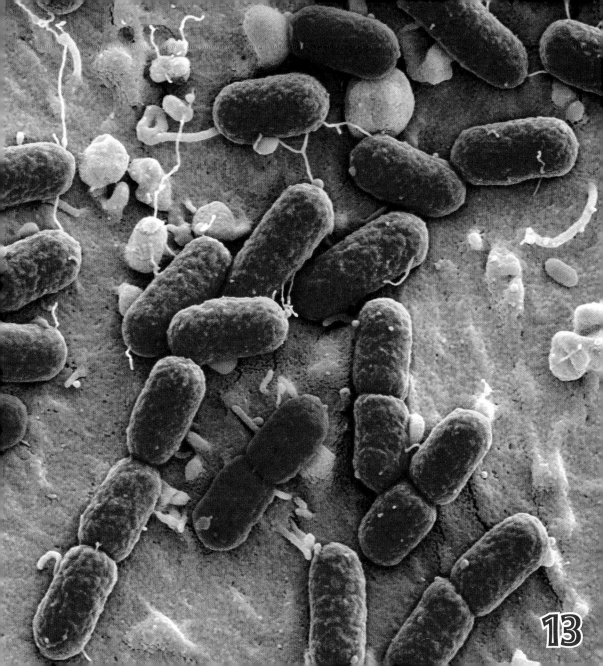

Sometimes you throw up from overeating—such as when you eat too much cake and ice cream during your birthday party. You may also throw up from eating two foods that don't go well together, such as spicy chicken wings and orange juice!

15

Have you ever felt like you were going to throw up after spinning around in a circle or riding in a car? That's called motion sickness. This happens when what the brain sees and what it feels don't match.

17

Take Care of Yourself

Some illnesses can cause you to throw up many times in a few hours. This causes the body to lose a lot of water, so it's important to replace it. If you can't stop vomiting or your vomit is red, you should go to the doctor.

PROBLEMS CAUSED BY FREQUENT VOMITING

- bile harms the teeth
- body can lose too much water
- may hurt the muscles of the digestive system
- vomit can enter the lungs
- may tear the tube between the mouth and the stomach

19

Animals Throw Up, Too

Many people know that animals, such as family pets, throw up when they're sick. Some dogs eat so fast that they throw up. Many animals, particularly birds, throw up for a totally different reason. They do it to feed their young! Now *that's* gross!

21

Glossary

digestive system: the parts of the body that work together to digest, or break down, food

fluid: something that is watery and flows like a liquid

germ: a tiny creature that can cause disease

muscle: one of the parts of the body that allow movement

For More Information

Books

Amsel, Sheri. *The Everything Kids' Human Body Book.* Avon, MA: Adams Media, 2012.

Miller, Connie Colwell. *The Pukey Book of Vomit.* Mankato, MN: Capstone Press, 2010.

Websites

KidsHealth
kidshealth.org/kid
Find more information about throwing up and many other health topics.

Need to Throw Up
www.pediatriconcall.com/kidscorner/whywhat/vomit.aspx
Learn more about why we throw up.

Index